animals

Photography
George Siede and Donna Preis

Louis Weber, C.E.O.
Publications International, Ltd.
7373 North Cicero Avenue
Lincolnwood, Illinois 60646

ISBN 0–7853–1281–1

Publications International, Ltd.

dogs

cats

rabbits

ducks

parakeets

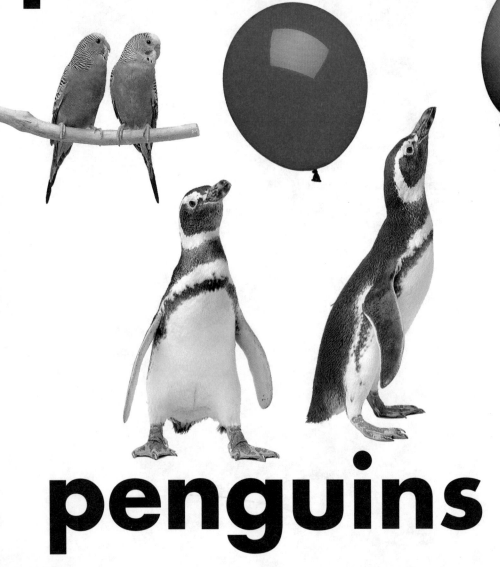

penguins

chickens

raccoon

monkey

frog

toad

turtle

goats

pigs

butterflies

fish